T0160911

ACTION IN THE ORCHARDS

ACTION
IN THE
ORCHARDS

FRED SCHMALZ

NIGHTBOAT BOOKS
NEW YORK

Copyright ©2019 Fred Schmalz

Printed in the United States

ISBN: 978-1-937658-98-4

Design and typesetting by adam b. bohannon

Text set in Adobe Garamond

Cover Art: Alex Yudzon, "Cobh Tree" (2017). Archival pigment print.

Interior Art: Deb Sokolow, "People Don't Like to Read Art" (2009). Graphite, ink, acrylic,

collage on bristol board.

Cataloging-in-publication data is available from the Library of Congress

Nightboat Books

New York

www.nightboat.org

CONTENTS

• • •

Documenta 13 daybook

• • • •

YOU'VE BEEN TOLD THAT PEOPLE DON'T LIKE TO READ ART, MAYBE
BECAUSE IT'S REALLY JUST SUPPOSED TO BE ABOUT IMAGES AND FIELDS
OF COLOR AND THAT SORT OF THING, AND ▓▓▓ WELL HELL, COME TO THINK OF IT,
YOU DON'T LIKE TO READ ART EITHER, NOPE, NOT AT ALL, BECAUSE IF YOU'RE GOING
TO SPEND YOUR TIME READING, IT MIGHT AS WELL BE A BOOK SO THAT LATER
ON WHEN PEOPLE ASK, "WHAT'VE YOU BEEN READING THESE DAYS?" YOU
CAN MENTION THE BOOK AND HOW GOOD IT WAS. ▓▓▓▓▓▓▓▓▓▓

EVEN IF IT WASN'T.

BIRDSONG TRUMPS DUMP TRUCK

birdsong trumps dump truck
pinkening the eastern sky

body in motion
tend to this day without end

bearing a bowl of rice as birds
distinct from clay flute

throat away in the gutters
bowl of salt

and birds we eat
I am restless expecting

mist to wrest free
these clouds and spoil

or make the afternoon
there are always better

options than the ones chosen
when I open this

orange I offer
the scent of oranges

1

canyons
crayons

like a chair
broken against the wall

then sunken into
I welcome you

when it is me
who arrives

GUIDED TOURS

show us a pageant
a wedding a minute

the first
Thanksgiving apartment

buildings on rocky hillsides
leading down to the sea

the price of a taxi
length of a squabble

the line forms around us
yet somehow excludes us

show us muddy boots that
slick path to the bus

stop from the warehouse
the benches and tables

you can't take home
what you found in the bushes

a harmonica a flower
the ability to orgasm

fear of minerals   plants
it is customary to ask

what animal would you be
were you not human

put this under your tongue
follow me into the river

AFTER ETEL ADNAN

I would like to wander
amid the heavens' explosions
a mountainous country's
nomadic art immaterial
if learned by heart
you move all the time
taking nothing with you
to meet the poets
from Kandahar and Kabul
replace philosophy
condensed essentially
says most at highest speed
sensed before thought
sometimes in the evening
after a party you go
into something ephemeral
the road to the city
accompanying Jew's harp
a strange attentiveness
reprograms us
to think through the thing
and by looking
deal thought
a blow for colors
as a means to say

what I can't
otherwise thoughts form
the core of objects
those shoes are blue
impossible to discuss
which is where
I have always been
sensitive to the weather
as such
yesterday I barely left bed
my body crumpled organ by organ
this is my deformity
interspatial comet crossing
stints as sleeper and slept
weeper and wept over
clocks can be fixed
there is no easy way to maintain
interest in the eternal

LANDING ON WATER

You asked me to meet you some place I had

never been, but imagined arriving,

was surprised to find it across the street,

entered anyway figuring you would

come along any minute. Outside ashes

pile up. The little sea on the sidewalk

hurdled or hurtled into unaware,

drenched, wobbling like a stick-legged doe.

I'm not the man who climbs outside guy wires

for the death rush. More triumphant to me

is the story of the French elephant

surviving the drop from a hovering

train to the river. I would have given

anything to be standing on the bank.

SOME ANIMALS

Here are some animals
I don't know what they are
Some are purple some white
Some have two dots for eyes
I don't know if they see
None have knees
They don't know what they are
Yet they got here
Some face right others left
Here are two animals snout to snout
Some are on hills or in valleys
Here is a rice paddy embedded in a hillside
I don't think rice grows here
Or the animals ate it
The purple ones with their snouts
Here are some cats
I know what they are but not how they will act
They are finished growing for now
Here are some hours
I don't know what they hold
Here are some minutes whose snouts nearly touch
Here days have no knees
Some days are purple and I never know in advance
Here is a live bat
I pulled it from under the skin on my cheek

Here a blemish grew black and unfurled its wings
Here is a hole where I fostered the bat
I didn't know what it was when it was under my skin
Here is where it bit my hand in the dead night
I picked it up in a white handkerchief
Its teeth are soft to the touch

THE CENTER OF ALL EUROPE

Song for held breath

Tell me the myth of smallness.
The only myth is greatness.
Then tell me how we go undetected.

*

Habits form that must be quit

The route over the river
takes me into the next town
past its new school building.

A map of Europe
hangs over the empty desks—
the sun in Andalusia.
The sun in Norway.

*

Charm for travel

Riled sleeper, the earth
is full of holes

pointing up. It is also
veined with paths.

*

In any direction the way is clear

Sea's here
but the sea
the locals visit
lies an hour south.

I said what I did
using few words
readily retrieved:
Island   Dock
The rest was stutter.

I could not
convey the breeze,
how it covered
us on the cliff,
how looking out was
in a way
looking down.

*

Goodbye, border patrol

We have to go to Poland,
it's like another planet—
the hotel furnishings
there aren't any curtains at all
any clothes.
Tripedals dance in the garden
the sound you hear scratched out
is the sound of hoopla
changing costumes
behind a tree
from nude skin to faun fur.

*

Lifting all boats

Stepping out of buildings
cycling through floods—
my face replaced by deluge,
my history in mud.

*

Double the price

The sculptor arrived at the scene

eating ice cream. Water
puddled everywhere around
wreckage of hinges, swollen
sprung cage of ancient doors.

A great wind transformed it.
"I cannot make what the elements
made here," its top
twisted into a nautilus
shell, its base a cracked bell,

surely it made a sound
as it fell, but it was late,
we slept through it all.

*

Habits form that must be quit

Lie still long enough
the shadows get you,
the showers.
It must be a comfort
to the farmer
in his tan raincoat
and fur-lined boots
who walks toward the wooden shed
but never reaches its door.

*

The only spinning vacancy

There is a town
not far from here
where a well
turned overnight
to salt water.

I shake rain off my bike.
Blue patches of sky appear.

*

The past is safe here

I can't place the tune
the white-haired woman downstairs
squeezes from her accordion,
but standing in the pantry
I make out through buckled tongue-
and-groove the catch-and-release
fingers on keys the instant
before chords change.
We learn slowly,
never remember enough.

*

The boundaries of the body are ropes

The glowing happens
whether or not
my neighbor is alive,
enough to lift her atrophied left
eyelid from her tea cup;

these colored balls
hung all over the house
so she thinks
we will follow her into history.

*

Last judgment

You are felled
by a felled tree.

JULIUS CAESAR GALLERY

Build bridge, cross and tear it down behind me.
I am one of fourteen disembodied heads
sharing portholes with a Roman column.
Music stand acts as sundial. We cross the Rhine.
We cross the Chicago River. Our necks
reflect the mechanics of barge bridges.
Come to me history. Let me eat from the salt night,
at my table dining with friends—define wind,
a well-known heavenly region, moveable, bruhmal.
Lying beneath the sun, ether born in loud shout
noticed behind other winds, a late bloomer.
From the chest up: paper. His inmost recesses
exposed to whirling in extremities.
Driven by the dog star from my encampment,
who will shudder me in the absence of salt?
It fills my mouth and I through it speak.

VOLERY

a woman sent out to gather
fog in her apron

warns you to stop getting pregnant
to eat a bird you have to

eat its feathers first
I am tired of stopping

to think the easy life
is the place my foot

lands between a humid morning's
shallow two shadows

our many back and forths
nourished on rust and whispering

scatter our laughter
a tincture of our own

darkness in brown glass
tells us it would be

fatal to settle in a city
the sky is not safe

if we are not tethered
weightless as we are

heaved through it
foolish enough to believe

we'll come unraveled
by our inability to quit

in the face of joy
the known feared

more than fear of flight
or flight itself, so flee

SURFACE TENSION

Get a new math

Echoes of terriers in a blind alley…
Listen and repeat:
instances reverberate, so we carry
silence unsteadily. There are
omens we haven't yet hatched.

*

Listen and repeat

In the provision for chance
all the music happens.
A lady's pair of shoes click
in the courtyard. She drops
wine bottles in a rubber tub.
We reach our hands out,
not to stop her
but to grace the act.

*

Our ears are now in excellent condition

No end to the noises. They supersede:
four sources of jack-hammering,
one circular saw.
If bricks were shorn clean,
we'd have a temple
erected on the cobbled shore.

*

Ignorances you are not guilty of

Your doctor tells you
if you see 74 movies
this week you won't miss
the sun so acutely.

He is like you in that
mistakes bother him
only when they are his own.

*

It's built-in that you can alternate

When you stand in the middle of a room
you are negligible.

Falling through space
you are something of a celebrity.
Little stars of the impossible shine for you.

*

Think of one

Lug a box across town
laden to rupturing with musk melons.
Your nervous system incorporates
limp into a form of *walk*—
you are on your way, you tell yourself.
Your feet carry on like gossip,
to a kitchen blender: enter
fruit, ice, milk. Think of one
once tasted. Her? Yes, her.

*

A foolish maneuver takes the heater by surprise

It is not right to lie
about the hole in your floor,
how it got there or why.
Your attempts to cover it
in linoleum only made
the rupture more obvious.

*

Fred, so help me . . .

I am over here and you are part of a distant
conversation. You are going to cry and you don't know it.
Nobody knows better
this calculus to loneliness:
we are invisible to those who may harm us—
each of us daring the first to step
and nobody moving a muscle.

*

Evidence

Somebody leans from a low bed
to peer through a blind, or bully
a locked door unlocked.
From these actions, a story emerges:
I slam a door and a mirror
falls off the opposite wall.
I keep my castle full with radios,
absorb a soaking new year's storm
and slowly return to dry,
this water-filled air mattress beneath me.

*

A reason offered for or against something

The air calmed and everyone lowered
their umbrellas.

When we leave,
we are manifestations of loss
as much as we are moving tokens.

When we pass from timepiece to ornament,
we should wrap this up and take cover.
It is a window. It will close.
We can make it back by dark.

*

The body warms and the body lets go

You move among tall pines
desiring nothing
but the lower back of a woman
whose body continues elsewhere
without your fixation
an independence likened to imagining
but free of attachments—
Was that her? No, another.
Recall: you have been spared
recognition by design. Your longing

returns as surprise:
the moment the history
you roll up behind you
becomes the plank you're walking.

*

How many homes do we need?

In another hour, the last split
among many possible wholes:
the end feels further away
further than ever.
I am not hungry but
there is room in my bag for more butter,
more honey and clover.

*

Closer to you is closer to the door

In a glass booth I hold my hand
before a candle and its warmth wraps around me.
A twist is simple. A body
given hands is not simple.
To be above water and swimming at once—
lifted from the ground and running.

*

The following classmates are lost . . .

Good for them.
Observe: you have been absorbed.
Sounds carry in this humidity, this heat:
the heavy door I hear clearly across the street.
Who is able to function in a life full of losses,
who doesn't ruin a walk in the woods
with visions of other locales?
This is your last last chance to join us…
Why are we still waiting for this light?

FLUX

the undetermined future
nightfall blocks out
other possibilities
gather at the stage door

last inklings slow me
through barricade raised
forced through as open range
in arbor hung inverted

to the searing
last moment of air
particulate air
slowing a spot found

on a wall in the wing
green rectangular light
balance held at speed
the road doesn't waver

but turns over in its carriage
in an ill-fitted suit
statisticians replace my shoes

a cement block breaks
tree trunks to rubble piled

neatly nightly by stagehands
I can smell myself

salt-stained white
coastline dampered marimba
questions deferred like
who do you live with

how can you trap the sky
in its present state I act
as though every day is
unable to catch me

STUDIO MUSEUM

One arrives by bus as one
arrives on foot, overshot
two avenues if not off early
trundling eastward in landing gear
touchdown, in rollerskate
suitcase, and one is imminently
hungry. That's me and my lover
in the doorway recess eating
pizza carried overland in tinfoil.
In the photo of this street, we'd be
whited out, not erased from history
so much as burnt through
onto volcanic rock, our gold
arms and gold fists lead us
to the podium as if we are a bannister.

"I have made no sound," the sound said.
We eat and are eaten by the scene
before we retire to rooms above
street level, din still audible, at bay.
We are wise to walk back among
presents the past pulled from
a multitude. The fantastic sneak:
dawn's erosion into full-blown light,
hours from what you call "Young Evening,"

a post-dusk transference, blues' send off.
But this, this is noon and one arrives
wide open. We woke among livestock,
reaching in time a commonplace humanness,
should we ever need to unwrap it.

TWELVE TWOMBLYS (LEPANTO 2001)

Land and roll around on a cold cigar.

Sleep the dead's sleep from Rome to Carthage and back by
   another route.

Move rotting planters over gravel, rotting ships over reefs.

Film a woman in a scarf emptying staves of their musical
   notation.

One day and its successor entangle.

Art and anarchy, bait thrown into the water. For anonymity's
   sake (Conjure and disappear!)

Every painter knows three lies: repeat after me.

I am the burning sun, the spider's dance over water.

(Conjure and disappear! Disappear!)

The man I didn't tell haunts me to Venice and back.

Sandals wear down the road, boats strain at their moorings—
    they leave in the morning.

I am named after a park bench that was in turn named in my honor.

NEW MUSEUM (INSIDE)

Be you book quote or lambchop,
be you cactus or couch, cold beer
in band box be you son absorbing
a lifetime of mother's spittle-fleck,
this hurts me more than you,
parakeet, this hurts be you
Hester Prynne or Sigur Ros, be you
archive egg or antidote to longing.
See how we look at layer on layer
of butterflies see how we have
so many windows open we freeze,
be you mattress or fatigue,

chaos come browsing
for its specimens in office corridors,
in image searches labeled 'terminal'
and 'luminous.' Be you limitation
on a great knowledge, be you voyager
shot down by missiles for being
revolutionary and loving flowers.

I AM A CAMERA

Melodies go to my stomach.
Have I missed something?
Staged for the dubious items:
murky memoirs, noise and alcohol,
quite a story to me and even more to her.
Everything that happened was nothing.
I was broke. Money was short
by new year's eve. I stood by the bust
of a Prussian general staring through a window
at signs of hope and comfort:
a fur stole, a coal wagon.
Like a widow I mirrored inflation.

We had idealized our promises to the new.
Innocence, a fresh scent opened,
but she, I think, does not yet know
where the lilac hangs, how old the world
was when we met.
A minute later, she wasn't there.
The look of the eyes is not love.
Nor is it a sixth sense. She remembered
my attention to conflict. I have a heart
defenseless by night. The hour came
and passed. Bravery did no good.
I supposed points of resemblance

were: pupil, curtain, light switch,
word play. An absolute dream
shocks. See you later. Yes, see you
in no uncertain terms. Partitions.
From her case a cascade of flatware
lifted from the widening mire.
We could have been just deep in love.
Troubling the difference lit from behind
apartment blocks overlooking the lake.
Tonic on tonic taken for hair
loss and cough. I will never be the same,
I've got rather too much vitality already.

CLAES OLDENBURG'S FESTIVAL OF LIVING OBJECTS
(THE STORE I)

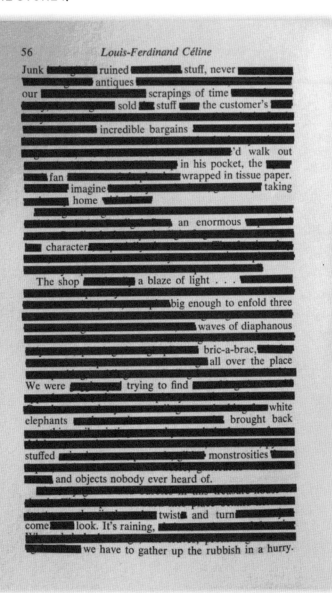

56   *Louis-Ferdinand Céline*

Junk ▮▮▮▮ ruined ▮▮▮▮ stuff, never ▮▮▮▮
▮▮▮▮ antiques ▮▮▮▮
our ▮▮▮▮ scrapings of time ▮▮▮▮
▮▮▮▮ sold ▮ stuff ▮ the customer's ▮▮

▮▮▮▮ incredible bargains ▮▮▮▮

▮▮▮▮ 'd walk out
▮▮▮▮ in his pocket, the ▮▮
▮▮ fan ▮▮▮▮ wrapped in tissue paper.
▮▮ imagine ▮▮▮▮ taking
▮▮ home ▮▮

▮▮▮▮ an enormous ▮▮

▮▮ character ▮▮▮▮

The shop ▮▮▮▮ a blaze of light . . . ▮▮

▮▮▮▮ big enough to enfold three

▮▮▮▮ waves of diaphanous

▮▮▮▮ bric-a-brac, ▮▮
▮▮ all over the place

We were ▮▮▮▮ trying to find ▮▮▮▮

▮▮▮▮ white
elephants ▮▮▮▮ brought back

stuffed ▮▮▮▮ monstrosities ▮

▮▮ and objects nobody ever heard of.

▮▮▮▮ twist ▮ and turn ▮▮
come ▮▮ look. It's raining, ▮▮▮▮

▮▮▮▮ we have to gather up the rubbish in a hurry.

CLAES OLDENBURG'S FESTIVAL OF LIVING OBJECTS
(THE STORE II)

We crawl around on our knees, scraping under ▮▮▮ furni-
ture. ▮▮▮▮▮▮▮▮▮▮▮▮▮▮▮▮▮▮▮▮▮▮▮▮▮▮▮▮▮
▮▮▮▮▮▮▮▮▮▮▮▮▮ cut glass▮▮▮▮▮▮▮▮▮▮▮▮▮▮▮▮▮
▮▮▮▮▮▮▮▮▮▮▮▮▮▮▮▮▮▮▮

▮▮▮▮▮▮▮▮▮▮ the furtive customer ▮▮▮▮▮▮▮▮▮▮▮▮
▮▮▮▮▮▮▮▮▮▮▮▮ explains his business▮▮▮▮▮▮▮▮
he has a small object to sell.▮▮▮▮▮▮▮▮▮▮▮▮▮▮▮▮
▮▮▮▮▮▮▮▮▮▮▮▮▮▮▮▮▮▮▮▮▮▮▮▮▮▮▮▮▮
▮▮▮▮▮▮▮▮▮▮▮▮ the kitchen sink▮▮▮▮▮▮▮▮▮▮▮▮▮
▮▮▮▮▮▮ He leaves ▮▮▮▮▮▮▮▮▮▮▮▮▮▮▮▮▮▮▮
▮▮▮▮▮▮▮▮▮▮▮▮▮▮▮▮▮▮▮▮▮▮▮▮▮ the
shop.
▮▮▮▮▮▮▮▮▮▮▮▮▮▮▮▮▮▮▮▮▮▮▮▮ looking ▮▮
▮▮▮▮▮▮▮▮▮▮ on edge. ▮▮▮▮▮▮▮▮▮▮▮▮▮▮
▮▮▮▮▮▮▮▮▮▮▮▮▮▮▮▮▮▮▮▮▮▮▮▮▮▮▮▮▮

▮▮▮▮▮▮▮▮▮▮▮▮▮ in the shop. ▮▮▮▮▮▮▮▮▮
▮▮▮▮▮▮▮▮▮▮▮▮▮▮▮▮▮▮ some ▮▮▮▮▮ mess.
▮▮▮▮▮▮▮▮▮▮▮▮ we sat still▮▮▮▮▮▮▮▮ a little
▮▮▮▮▮▮▮▮▮▮▮▮▮▮▮▮▮▮▮▮▮▮▮▮▮▮▮▮▮
▮▮▮▮▮▮▮▮▮▮▮▮▮▮▮▮▮▮▮▮▮▮▮▮▮▮▮▮▮
▮▮▮▮▮▮▮▮▮▮▮▮▮▮▮▮▮▮▮▮▮▮▮▮▮▮▮▮▮
▮▮▮▮▮▮▮▮ gas jet ▮▮▮▮▮▮▮▮▮▮▮▮▮
in darkness. ▮▮▮▮▮▮▮▮▮▮▮▮▮helped ▮▮▮▮▮▮
▮▮▮▮▮▮▮▮ to encourage us ▮▮▮ It took ▮▮▮▮▮
red wine▮▮▮▮▮▮▮▮▮▮▮▮▮▮▮▮
and ▮▮ storing ▮▮ junk . . . ▮▮▮▮▮▮ heaps of ▮▮
▮▮▮▮▮▮▮ stuff that ▮▮▮▮▮▮▮▮▮▮▮▮▮
could▮▮ be sold, ▮▮▮▮▮▮▮▮▮▮▮▮▮▮▮▮▮
▮▮▮▮▮▮▮▮ From the transom ▮▮▮▮▮ hung down ▮▮
▮▮▮▮▮▮▮▮▮▮▮an enormous hood that took up half the
room. In the end ▮▮▮▮▮▮▮▮▮▮▮▮▮▮▮▮▮
▮▮▮▮▮
It was like living in a filthy museum.
▮▮▮▮▮▮▮▮▮▮▮▮▮▮▮▮▮▮▮▮▮▮▮▮▮▮▮▮▮

CLAES OLDENBURG'S FESTIVAL OF LIVING OBJECTS (THE STORE III)

He was there in the shop ▮
Draped in his finery ▮
he'd make paper birds ▮

every night he started ▮ adding new
touches. ▮

the Gallery of Machines. ▮ was terrifying!
Hanging in midair ▮
way up to the sky. ▮

were giant ▮ gleaming

rigged up ▮
rows of enormous cakes, fantastic
cream puffs, ▮
flags, ▮ light bulbs

soft ▮ wrapped up in ▮ furs.

there was nothing else in the world. ▮

Between us and ▮ a riot

HOTEL (RECORD)

woman who sighs for a living   remains obscured   faint coco-
nut melting plastic   another half hour skates past   kneesocks
woman who sighs for a living enters hotel   no intention of
checking out   my chair doesn't exist   fire embers   dangers stem
from exposure   demise   root burnt cave   faint coconut melt-
ing plastic   fry feathers   coals wane ember out   hell's trap door
boy with plumage wanders over   descendent among neighbors
snakes amidst great men apologize for ills   pale sheep sneak
through vale   glow in the dark   plastic monsters chew my
hair   pull chain   motorcycle kickstart suitcase strap rack   walk
across east side   pluck luggage unattended   can anyone give
me two nickels for a dime   damned 55-cent payphone   table
reserved   man leans into me   smell breath   temple   melting
plastic   island within another island   woman sighs for a liv-
ing returns me safely   woman six months pregnant contracting
already late   call doctor   wrecks car against light pole backs
up wrecks against light pole backs up wrecks wreckage against
light pole backs up wrecks light pole after light pole   grill bent
faint palm oil ember   rubber   release clear   we hear trashmen
steam drills subside   sheep throats spring blood   dinner served
knock-kneed maiden rushes door   melts nooses   rain follows
fear rain unaccounted   storm scuttles me   wills back those
around me   enter hotel   rooms offer sponge bandage chair
faint palm oil ember   ember   passionate a sundial   unpacked

45

THE DEAD OF WINTER

I had not felt so
tired so early in the day
since last winter

when we lived apart
for a time and the light
fixtures failed one by one

I grew accustomed to the dim
hallway the way the study
became after four a kind of
mausoleum until dawn

I shed all appearances
there was nothing
stopping me from sleeping
altogether

only the occasional
wrong number dialed
the regular deliveries

I will sort them out later
I thought
if ever

DEMOLISHING THE BURNED HOUSE

today's word   *dust*
super-ceiling   sub-floor
live in us
independent our invitation
retell upbringings
leaving the deaths in
an arrangement where
everyone gets younger
news given grace
broken   even
as the love of my life
found in grammar unintended
meant to say meet me
hear   mean   echo fell
bereft in faint light
blue television on
with no one there
no absolute silence
body machine whirring
teeth struck together
musically   crystalline
water   water
door jarred   axe
this was never my era
in the first place

WOMAN SINGING IN A MAN'S VOICE

all fairy tales
are about sex
telescoping

inside me   your hand
moves like a kite
pretty   endowed

with a knack for lust
oceans   accidents of birth
forlorn   waving

flashlights
deep in a forest
the woods are fake

it's the wolves
that are real
plainly   visible

still qualifying
as artificial
motor functions

bent into questions
through slight miscalculation
                    grotesque

like any house
smaller the longer
its lived in

tracts overgrown
with rushes
                jonquil

june flower
violet   beguiling
coat cut

from a bolt of black cloth
cold that sidles up
an oblation to chainsaws

DOOR IN A BATH

hatchling
every touched surface
inherits us

the daily mail
approximates birds
we were all so

moving hoofing
among rooftops

tin eye
wind abated

clinging sideways
to a tree's face
a warm hum by the time

the hole it goes into
misses us dearly

*

after you
didn't answer

I imagined you   motionless
        in the tub

I joked
last week was
big enough
you can drown in it

                *

this letter waited a year
long enough   could be
about anything
missing great patches
in formation   codex

all this grammar   implanted
divisible by any number mumbled
                must be my prime

                *

when will it be
safe to try again
what have I done
without that
now seems necessary

I have to
move all the time
is the air
clung to me

        *

talk through water
     bags
on both feet   a suitcase
opened flat
inside it   rectangular lawns

see in the sky
        undressed
     colors eaten
by other   wetter   colors

        *

the edges disappear
relief   a hole lit

I look like a cage
I am not a cage
nor do I resemble freedom

I forgot to tell you
I neglected to say

a sea cut open
reveals another sea

*

no feeling
about death
until just now

now what

the rest of
the day

tiny sails
carry me
across a pond

*

the lap in the bay
perfumed in hyacinth

waiting to be formed
by the rough hand of summer

THE KNIFE

assumes god reneges
on me slowly if and when

I don't stay still
something's fallen down

a boat being bailed
while it fills from the hull

separating arrivals from times
I stayed put   no mystery why

the highway bypasses this place
cold roots it out

in shaded water
mirage repeating to the horizon

apparition vanishing
silver in the sky

past fences the last undrained
birthmark beneath the dam

what was lake apparition
vanishing droughted dry

pierced by gold daisies
slowly if and when

I speak about the knife
all of us are under

I AM A DEAD ARTIST

At the moment this title is wrong.
A very long time ago my parents made love
one minute before, ten seconds before
I was made in this time,
born in the 20th century—

a different period in my life.
From the beginning, a trauma.
When you go there you feel absence—
one night in our room
I tried to pass a long time lying on my bed watching TV. It
    wasn't easy.

Perhaps you will understand a long, slow psychoanalysis:
When I was young I was sad, nearly crazy
I stopped school at 12, made a drawing
more happy at the end than at the beginning.
I became an adult when I was 23

in one minute my childhood finished
300 years ago, 400 years ago
someone played music
a new incarnation each time
the same and not the same

each time permanent strange.
Often I have nothing to do—
sometimes the wall opens,
sometimes I have no face but a mirror.
Each time I fail to save against memory—

when I die no one will remember my grandmother.
Fifty years dissipates quickly—
the people who die or are born in one day.
I am going to die in three years.
If I die in ten, terrible,

if I die tonight crossing the street
I told you before:
tomorrow I must take the train.
Tomorrow I have an eye exam.
At the end we are good and bad

when you are an artist
you can be happy one night thinking it is good what you made.
Often you have no name but a number
at the time of you-never-know.
If we wait some years the title will be true.

DOCUMENTA 13 DAYBOOK

DAY -477: GEOFFREY FARMER, PRELUDE TO "LEAVES OF GRASS"

bring me the art stars of tomorrow
bring me their handbags

their horse sees a four-frame film
in line for *The Clock* New York awakes to

black and white educational television
held together with string wire spot of tape

that's never going to stay fast
while we crash Chelsea leaves

the last of its love to you lovelies
if there is a trend toward quantum physics

we have a choice gift me the ghost
its getting warmer and I can't escape

last night's waitress the unsettling air
reminds me of her four distinct lines

she has a family she is a figure
uncomplicated with tiny ankles for each

of her six feet a collage of beauty
and death of course looks cool

ripped from the pages of *LIFE*
I like *LIFE* am trying to be revolutionary

in my manners I think a drink
would help us get a word in edgewise

— Christian 6.7.12

— João 26.8.12

— Erica 25.8.12   — Donna 12.9.12
          — José 29.6.12
— Laura 28.6.12   — [   ] 12.6.12
     — Ryan 31.8.12   — Jason 11.8.12
— John 23.8.12   — Julian 2.8.12
— Madeline 15.7.12   — Marleen 11.8.12
— Eva 14.7.12   — Sarah 24.8.12
     — Daniela 2.8.12 — Laja 11.6.12 — Ekaterine 11.8.12
— Rachel 3.8.12   — Susan 8.7.12   — Bärbel 15.7.12
                    — Emily 16.6.12
— Uljana 7.7.12

bicycle   umbrella   unlimited pass

DAY 62: SANJA IVEKOVIĆ "THE DISOBEDIENTS (THE REVOLUTIONARIES)"

I am the subject of your objectification
subjected to your objects while
I objectify our objects' subjectivity
if I am an object of your study
I take the subject from your stance
you have it however you like
I am a stuffed donkey
studied indirectly I am
understood to raise a hand
to what is objectionable
among the array of objects
presented   given
time to subject to scrutiny
the rarified air to which we repair
crackle of the p.a. system
if there are no further questions
my assistant will present the subjects
if there are no objections
the objects will also be presented

DAY 98: FRIEDRICHSPLATZ

I lived five years
in this town

a man waiting for his arm
to grow back

DAY 5: MICHAEL PORTNOY "27 GNOSIS"

every evening a call to prayer
when long afternoons' light
felt an unmovable force
in search of objects
stopped at crossings
(urge to smash glass)
I don't want to tell you
how I hated the thought
we must fit
into the world lived by others
(often voices concur)
whether we understand or not
maybe we are looking at
half of something
a draft   table knocked over
(urge to smash glass passed)
we have left
our intermittencies behind

DAY 8: LYDIA DAVIS AT STÄNDEHAUS

I am a door between
offices of lost objects

relate to me
a story about grief
a story a friend
on the high plains
gives   her first fir forests

I serve as
a box of raisins
tucked into a loaf of bread

DAY 88: THOMAS BAYRLE'S MACHINES, DOCUMENTA HALLE

what had I told you about
grace or fear of the unknown
cross wherever you like
a balance kept
longer than you

kept your fingers
(farm accident — implement)

a piston drops
rises repeatedly
consoled by the remaining
hand held tight
what I would give to be
audience to be watched

DAY 1: THEASTER GATES "12 BALLADS FOR HUGENOTTENHAUS"

long early sun come west
an orbiting body approaches
a suitcase full of glasses
a drawer of false teeth
with real teeth pulled
weathervane to help
quarter the weather

tomorrow it will rain
into a tub
lugged through the garden

one apartment noise emits confetti
mantel clock elicits unease

tremors hard to dissipate

The White Problem in America

where am I gone
who could be ready for that

DAY 7: AMAR KANWAR "THE SOVEREIGN FOREST"

open   opened
was opened
out into the sea

is it water or grass
cenotaph   series of maps
disputed land

twenty pylons intrude
my unpardonable landscape

ask the living about the dead
at umbrella point

she sees him in everything

if he says atlas he means maps
from his notebooks we can deduce
metronome survived
along with man
stepping over a plush settee
turning atlas
a woman on his back
if he says tome
he has reset his watch
to unsay to unremember
each new entrant
attempts to reposition a chair
but the chairs remain
bolted to the floor
the full stop swallows the sentence

DAY 2: KAI ALTHOFF "A LETTER TO CAROLYN CHRISTOV-BAKARGIEV"

her apology read
like a suicide note
only obliquely
returning to synchronicity

my father likes you
so much too

what I can say
however is
I don't know

or that lung
split in two
trying to clear
already empty rooms

freezes flames hung
from the banister between us
forms a perfect wave

DAY 84: MARK DION "XYLOTHEQUE KASSEL"

stars arranged as I would
a dinner table
graph affixed to the wall
determines when we will
all be free
to scare off cupid's ghost
the *i-ching* beyond me
started in a womb too
today I was born

DAY 82: JEANNO GAUSSI "FAMILY STORIES"

I walk away from myself
into nameless others

the statues are laughing

gathering
crowd
audience
mob

various ribbon cuttings

Bakshi and his students

the hand gestures
they employ when singing

am I still telling the story
pointless men tell

am I townie or train station

DAY 6: BLACK BOX, ORANGERIE

a floor that's all sky
box opaque
its function unknown
or lost
                    knowledge
its fragility
in storage
a 'sleeper'
                 prism
not born yet
transmits
all of space archived
fragmentary dispersed
obsolete
moved in pieces
a machine to measure
                        providence
let happen

magnet meets metal shavings
chasing each other here
I am here I am
barbed wire unconvinced
I keep anything out

combustion   paper   bellows
subscribers to private orchestras
a red   X   drawn and me crosshaired

entropy drops down a well
tidy
transforms what one thought
known into counter-clock-
wise clock hands

resistance to handy thesis

the fevered dream
of what was to come

DAY 8: PIER PAOLO PASOLINI "SALO O LE 129
GIORNATE DI SODOMA"

three bowls arranged
into a row before us
I am tempted to name them
you name them
grass grown knee high
holds out for winter
tamp downs field mice
then snakes pregnant
with field mice
a dog with a snake
hanging loose from its muzzle
retrieval of stones
ferried home in a girl's shirt
smooth from brook runs
I am tempted to name them

DAY 25: TACITA DEAN "FATIGUES"

entering a theater
intent on falling asleep
a man sits next to a woman
speaks slowly uninterrupted
beyond cognizance

confluence flash flood
ice floe
upper air
antediluvian
pincer movement (imagined)
snow (on view)
in prevailing direction
tense erasure

the ride home
his conscience sears

DAY 78: FRIEDRICHSTRASSE

dear diary my friends
are in the house
while I am outside
getting greener by the turn
dear diary I miss them
so naturally I think
it might be whooping cough
or the soup I reheated
before that walk
through the forest

DAY 19: PIERRE HUYGHE "UNTILLED"

reaching the last
herd of goldfinch
the eye of the storm
is over me

this weather drinkable
if drinking
is an option
ask for a bit to bite
or a drip to drowse you

overlooking roads' remains
graveyard of car parts
used speed bumps
guides to behavior
I have no repercussion

hemmed in
grateful for guidance
bees
congregate on the garden gate

DAY 30: TINO SEHGAL "THIS VARIATION"

it rains so we dip into the canal
Carrie also sits rocking
but does so beyond the lobby

not the sound of nails
being dropped
but nails spread
across parquet

not the smell of glitter
but glitter
drying on a wall

a baby babbles over beaten boxes
enough to make me cry

DAY -1: KASSEL HAUPTBAHNHOF

receive and heed instruction
paint corrugated huts orange
blind spots furtive
lightbulb breakage
temple curtain torn asunder
mountain villages draw down
bed feathered by wayfinders
seep meets be seen panoptic
by the close of these hundred days
my money no good here

IN THE ABSENCE OF A BODY

eat breakfast with a man

who occasionally knocks

protected by the state

(if he cuts out

a durational act

in space both public and derelict

built for x, now used for y

a mark

exceeds us

sum of absences (still

a fold felled a shirt skirted

apart from soot stain

my legacy

on the other side of a vent

is a notional presence

takes no measure of his limits

silence (. . .)

between intentions

chairs all in the air

bring about his own demise

begun as testimony

(microphone knock)

behind a vent

dresses the part

three weeks' work negated

interiority

lamp emanating from the floor   tiresome illumination

sometimes I have to turn it off   *sit in the dark*

a spirit accumulated   tabula rasa

should become silent   mental (neural)

when all you have is a microphone   everything looks like a wall

one wind and swish   disappearing weightlessness

only air intends to escape   aftermaths matter (solid)

profanity (escapes)   to allow appearance anew

(the poets are)   invisible beyond

Void devoid   three ways impossible

science (eloquence)   the intersection

as ethos   (therefore funereal)

wall's spine   gathers drops of water

via microphone (puncture)

Shibboleth   Saragossa   CRACK

on second thought

to live on (consequences)

recesses

sheetrock shorn away

a right to interiority

bring him rooftops

as intense presence

(memory vacuum)

INHIBITION

When I hoped, I feared. When I feared, I dared

to measure an extraordinary

life against mine. When I break up the talk

I dream in whitewash, blank blackboard, in lips

moving without accompanying sound—

proof in itself I am getting smaller.

Soon I may disappear altogether.

Your presence is requested for this

procession toward early afternoon—

I am alone and the exits are locked.

Lovelier than I wanted, to admit

the air at the edge of my endurance.

Nothing drags me away. Still, I sleep with

arms out to make the lifting easier.

THE COUNTRY'S ONLY OPEN-AIR
MARBLE DANCE FLOOR

how I would have liked a stone to push off

my chest every morning so I would have

work to do before going back to bed

would have liked to mention how pain enters

leaving me infected not by angels

but earthly bodies: horns, visitations

by sirens into my silences hot

nights I thought I had to myself before

the call I would have given anything

to take back but instead it connected

harkening and recoiling its bell

tones I so long faltered in their absence

existing in a kind of orange talk

daring the air around me to come true

THE LINE ENDING FOREVER

At first the photo looked like New York
But I can see now it is here

I am not sure what street
The perspective shifted by light, foliage

The beauty of photos is not their faces
It is the way light flushes the corners

The sun rose between St. Martin's two green steeples
I left the hotel with three clementines in my jacket

I figured they would see me to dinner
By nightfall I was hungry

Here are some friends
Their beauty is in the light they flush into photos

                    *

They work together and live together
They have a long distance relationship

They met and within months were married
They were together for years but never married

Her family was uncomfortable with her choices
I don't know if it's permanent

They split after a year living apart
They visited every weekend

They drifted away from each other
They lived together the whole time

It wasn't that they didn't want to
They poked it with a stick but it didn't move

She tucked herself into bed with little hope of sleeping
If she were there they would be awake anyway

*

She called from China early in the morning
She was drunk and it was the day before

Last week she totaled her car at a stoplight
She was looking over her shoulder, not paying attention

She had a job but she was on lunch break
Her work gives her one hour

She cut her hair to get over him
Then grew it out, searching for another

*

The doorbell rang and her wedding ring arrived
The mail was three weeks later than expected

Yesterday she cried in the kitchen
Convinced it had been stolen

When valuables are broken, danger is averted
This does not extend to theft

So we may no longer be safe
Packages left unattended will be resold at auction

I should rent a room far away to avoid accidents
I leave earlier and earlier for work each day but traffic never eases

Someone moved out and left all their furniture leaning against
    the building
The sidewalk is barely passable

I couldn't tell if they had broken up or gotten together
Dawn resembles dusk in many respects

*

She wanted me to send a message from one light source to
    another
I gathered the sheet by its four corners

Held it to a lamp and read slowly
Many words were unclear

There was no pattern to my misunderstanding
The cut out parts were accentuated by a vellum overlay

Palilogy is the repetition of words for emphasis
A palimpsest

I passed her house on the way to the little pharmacy
She wanted me to walk her to work

It's hard for me to hold hands in public
Most days are remotely connected like today

I rarely spoke on the phone the months I lived apart
I forgot and numbness took hold

When I visited in the spring my sadness had not begun
My sadness came home while I was away

*

He was new here and never spoke
Until he proposed to her in a restaurant

He asked for everyone's attention
Something borrowed and returned

When he asked her she was hiding under the table
Everyone cried a little

She was moving away in the fall and feared getting attached
This made him nervous

He had to ask her old man
They took out the line ending forever hold your peace

At the party he kissed three men and four women
This was met with awkward silence

They waited and saw
She really did join the circus

She called when she landed
By then he slept in a corner of the house

Normally shuttered in winter
It qualified as something blue

OUR FORTUNES OUR FRIENDS

When we ask what our lives hold,
is it this? Are we wired
to recognize that other—
encountered in our plate-spinning days—
as a body coming closer?
We meet and go on meeting.

When within reach, we reach
as if our intersections
play out along a plain
plotted here and here and then
Oh, hello. The opening long sought.
We go orbiting each other.

You make me storm shelter
where the sky complies. Simply put:
I sleep uneasily when you're away. But
wasn't I ready for anything before?
We ask for mercy. That's finding another.
From there it's gravity and gardening,

which is itself an act of bravery: we till
and are rewarded with open earth,
leaving rogue heirlooms, sage
abundant to line our walk

long after we've decamped west.
Our smithereens sparkle—

Forms visceral in their beauty
orbiting each other as we
cluster the enamored, gather crowd
gather mason jars all sizes.
We come here to be covered
in apples—their red

glow suits us like a barn at midday—
all of it witness to the sustenance
that courses through us—olives and loaves,
Chateau Something-or-other, the birds
in the eaves. Our fortunes, our friends,
convince us there is a place for love,

a languorous intertwining that girds us
to admit love scares us while urging us to toil
together in a barrel of soil,
to coalesce around the meaning of *drum*
when I feel your sternum thrum at the song of thrushes
and to love that without measure.

UPBRINGINGS

someone is giving birth
on a mattress
it's raining
mattresses are being
delivered someone
is giving out
mattresses have
a boy or a girl
a can of hot fat
pours out a fry pan
do you have rain or father
your furniture your future
talisman

*

world of claws
marsh hawk trained
on eastern Oregon
high desert cattle ranch
the summer my father
dropped a running
chain saw across his thigh

*

multiply the west wild as you will
reach me regardless
vibrating on trigger wire
tensions wind around me
their detonations fail
today a bomb dropped on Kassel
69 years ago was found in the Fulda
authorities marked it with a buoy
the frontier ends here
rising among ordinance

*

insert as history how seriously
I took faith in god
that I worried two brown felt strips
emblazoned with images of saints
insert as shame I recall
nothing but two strings covering
breastbone and spine white
rosary black rosary wooden
confusion over the sequence of catechism
going to hell requires repetition
insert as host assumed absolution
whole heart blue carpeted
I was led in one day when it rained

pews removed to the sacristy
the following year the building
was a gravel patch in the parking lot

*

great uncle Geeg
accessory to armed robbery
knocked over an A&P
was caught
busted out of Joliet
three months shy of parole
was caught
took a side-gunner's spot
rather than return
his B-17 flacked down
over Schweinfurt
was caught
spent the war's balance
in Luftwaffe lock-up
went straight his remaining days
despite throwing
at his sister Jean
the occasional frozen fish
roped out of Lake Wauwautosee

*

great uncle Urban
is still tagged a ne'er-do-well
for reasons unexplained

*

solstice if you notice
appeals to me
my heirlooms vanish
in the hall mother
descends into a pile of jade
comes with solo flights
with bluffs blinded answers
no longer applicable once
I have thrown frozen peas
and mannequin torso
from the window
did I live under a cloud
panting at shades

*

I had migration and invisibility
on my side before I ran out of wire
if all families are divided
by their transience our futures
have no faces no lands end nor landfall
nor station into which we rumble

unassuming long after
the last connection embarks
this simplifies matters
our suitcases ourselves
that apple I dry on my sleeve
cut into quarters with a blunt blade
is apple to me standing in the hall
breath departing as I have
staked out a ritual for watched pots
while my famished animals brazenly hoof

WITHOUT YOU THERE IS NO LUNCH

every half hour
I stand up to
forget my past

to mother is a verb
to daughter
a never used

room full of strangers
encumbered with stones

I found little
to point to in fervor

how was it again
we were made wary
vague invites

say something mythological
like your body
in this fine crepe

how wilted
we have all grown
in the meantime

if not otherwise
or else

to ladle
leave me one good arm
to stew

FAMILY GHOSTS MEET THE INVENTION OF THE FUSE

In a manor house after breakfast
a man lies down in his quarters
face down, the door closed.

A figure appears in the door's place
holds steady, carries nothing,
overlooks his position, makes no request,

passes along the sconces:
smells pillow, bed sheet,
wall's concert bills and flight patterns—

constants purveyed,
liberation from futures our natures repel.
Pinned to the bed quivering

the man surveys
a minor intersection: haunt and hollow
bodies non-bodies bodies unseen—

getting on with things leaves
spirits marginal, impeded by impulses
electrical. Salt pure and simple.

*

Bring levity.
Levitate.
Pull levers electricians leave idle—

risk shorts and showers of sparks
for status, fall back on
family invention: the fuse.

State the obvious to swallows in the eaves—
pound along the cage's rim
wearing malleable tin as crown

conduct currents
send shock waves groundward
to the green tides

that roll up under the porch.
Trifle with negative ions
bound to birth mothers.

Wail but briefly, abandoning
sentiment for a swim in the river.
Return to find clothes tossed high in a tree.

Someone here teach step one.
Step one: draw darkly a mask for fright
rattling the brink—a licked battery for the ears,

tang the tongue conquers and subsides
lingers into later meals,
advocating our commands.

POSTCARD FROM THE COUNTRYSIDE

in a village
between here and home
a woman releases
herself over her lover

tied up in memory
certain movements—the car
door shutting   the hollowing
sound inside each of us

after a mistake
there was a time
I loved everything
associated with this street

went to great lengths
reassuring myself
it was only me
who had changed

this is the nature of invitation
it makes me feel
like a horse
in line for bread

I have a room in mind
as I have a lake when I think
Go around that lake
and come back to me

if I grant this knot
its inglorious unwinding
I can sit by the steps
lengthening like a debt

from this unnoticed
wing of the evening
something wonderful
is bound to happen

I can't get closer
without drawing attention
if I don't move
they'll never even notice
I'm gone

CLOUDLESS
(SUSAN MARSHALL AND COMPANY)

because jet exhaust doesn't count

the sky is clear

because the sky's white lines tangle

it is never clear to me

*   *

rumors start this way

leaves fall this way

raked off

discarded nudes

*   *

our states of undress

111

invite comparison

our marked bodies

their symmetries

(a forearm, a face)

*   *

arms' arguments

books' brocades

figures and frames:

cloudless reliquary
one scrubbed cloud
three strings

and you attached to each

*　　*

your wet thumb　　　　　　　　　　and forefinger

pinch lit wick　　　　　　　　　　　after lit wick

the room darkens

lumen by lumen

*　　*

pale　　　　　　　　one
blue　　　　　　　　cotton
cube　　　　　　　　tooth

*　　*

the way a draft　　　　　　　　　may carry

the space heater's charge　　　　　my way

I name each temperature

and each change in

temperature

*   *

the elements

are enemies

the elements

define in you

the arguments

*   *

resist the furniture—

step outside

snow

covers grass

and leaves

      me in the grass

          *   *

          I roll up the rug

you do it faster

          set a table for your bed—

a napkin blown overhead

          *   *

hunker and swallow

          shut your mouth

     hear the rabble behind you

          the private
          universe is here:
          to greet it
          you crack a book
          with a fan

balance a tea cup on an ass

                *   *

you are related to nature

                grass
                leaves
                snow   ladder
                                                  rung
                                                bell

                  I am not natural at all

                *   *

a man is led

                    past me

      shirt in his teeth

                  holes
                  in the earth
                  send
                  confetti to the sky

    (   )

*   *

water
fire
censor   dictionary's
                        natural
                enemies

*   *

a man being led

              as unit of measure

              (distance, not time)

thunder

                (distance not

                recumbent

      children yelling over the hourchime

                *   *

there is no back seat

                              no abridging the text

I am trying to keep the sound in

                         *   *

it's like breathing

                you are compelled to follow

                         my hand

                    is nowhere to hear

          inch along

                    kneel on a knuckle

                         *   *

a prone body   a body

lifted to rafter   on countermeasure

        sand bags, pulleys, simple machines

               I raise myself up to you

CLOSE QUARTERS

brick   brick   bricklayer
        brick

one carried over scaffold
crane   crane   operator

roof re-roofed
skylight now

further from sky
a ton   tonnage

how weighty strong
or stiff sun   world shouldered

gutted cellar to ceiling
grows from its gutter   an oak

door   next door
neighbors maneuver

into driveways
without complaint

souls compliant   appear

to love us   let us

loft a tarp into crispened evening
roll back their own

cover   to reveal dilapidation
world without burst pipes

amen   as in agreement

as in second language
meaning more lost than conveyed

hear creator as reactor
envision fallout

can't go back
every year the disrepair

hear despair   correct to disappear
depends on winter's

severity   surveys
homes   steps from the roadway

famished   hear furnished
pull up the last chair in the room

by this means   (these means)

wounded   wound in gauze

still too far away
to see clearly

in the calamine gloam
not a day stretches

toward its successors
but twilight's succor   my own reflection

the holding still one   replaced
with   way to go

or where they went
turned green   an abscess

in my absence   certain landmarks
visible from one direction   stand out

leave pets   plants
the perishable

ovations   moments of silence
greeted as granted

givens   offered without goading
I will hound the lost until found

This book records encounters with art. As much as it is informed by experiences, it is infused with people, many of whom make art. Because they are artists, most of them are known only by a small coterie of others. This neither enhances nor diminishes the power of their work—though it does render that work somewhat obscure. So, for context, a few introductions are in order.

The sources for "Birdsong trumps dump truck" were a small clay bowl received as a gift from the poet Jenny Browne and seeing dancer Julian Barnett perform in Johannes Wieland's "Portrait."

"Guided tours" grew out of conversations with dancers and choreographers Su-Wei Wu, Jason Jacobs, and Ekaterine Giorgadze, as well as a large meal for a group of near-strangers.

"After Etel Adnan" began at Adnan's artist talk at documenta 13, Ständehaus, Kassel June 22, 2012. The talk started at noon on a Saturday. Many attended. I left the talk unable to recall what she had said—it had permeated me instantaneously.

"Landing on water" nods to coffee in Berlin with poet and translator Jen Hayashida and what seemed an apocryphal tale about the *Schwebebahn* told by an unreliable narrator on the steps of the theater in Wuppertal months later.

"Some animals" grew from an illustrated letter sent by writer Sarah Manguso. The first two lines are hers.

"The center of all Europe" relates a constellation of

encounters with the art exhibition documenta 12, in Kassel, Germany, in August and September 2007. The poem's subtitles quote Ai Weiwei, Alice Notley, CK Rajan, and Sarah Fox.

"Julius Caesar Gallery" was written at a performance by Chicago theater-makers Matthew Goulish and Lin Hixson, "Caesar's Bridge," at Julius Caesar Gallery, November 2, 2014.

"Volery" includes encounters with the works of dancer and choreographer Elisabetta Lauro and photographer Addie Juell.

"Surface tension" references writings by John Cage, Brian Blanchfield, Harryette Mullen, and Jose Lezama Lima, songs by Thelonious Monk, and paintings by MP Landis. Its earliest versions were written for a collaboration with Landis one summer at the Fine Arts Work Center in Provincetown. Landis is a painter with excellent ears.

"Flux" draws from an encounter with an artwork from the inside—as performer. In choreographer Johannes Wieland's "Flux," I ran on a treadmill countersunk into the floor of the stage for the duration of the performance. People danced and strobe lights went off around me. Inverted trees descended from above the stage.

The inspiration for "Studio Museum" was a visit to New York with Susy Bielak, direct from LaGuardia to view Glenn Kaino's sculpture and the exhibition "When the Stars Begin to Fall" at the Studio Museum in Harlem in June 2014.

"Twelve Twomblys (Lepanto 2001)" began with a visit to Cy Twombly's paintings, drawings, and sculptures at the Brandhorst Collection in Munich. One semicircular room exhibits the twelve-painting, late-career work Lepanto, which is impossible to view all at once, since the first and last paintings are almost 180 degrees opposite each other. This visit came in the days leading up to the German marathon championships, in which I was a competitor. I was staying with the choreographer Ryan Mason, who lived at the time around the corner from Thomas Mann's house. I spent the mornings doing my last brief pre-race strides in front of the white wall around Mann's home.

The same 2014 visit to New York with Susy included a stop at the "New Museum (inside)," where we viewed Camille Henrot's video "Grosse Fatigue" and installation "Is it possible to be a revolutionary and like flowers," as well as Ragnar Kjartansson's "Me, My Mother, My Father, and I." That day, we ran into the poet Matthea Harvey and Rob Casper in the lobby, a true New York encounter. Three years later we shared a New Museum elevator with Yoko Ono. Susy leaned into her, smiled, and said, "It's so nice to see you," which is a poem I am still writing.

"I am a camera" follows Daniel Borzutzky's maxim of writing down what's happening on the television.

While conducting research for a series of gallery walks at the Walker Art Center in 2013, I learned that sculptor Claes Oldenburg had been reading the French novelist Louis-Ferdinand Céline's *Death on the Installment Plan* while creating his 1961 installation "The Store" in New York. "Claes Oldenburg's Festival of Living Objects" is my attempt to connect these two works.

"Woman singing in a man's voice" was written while attending an opera performance.

Artist Christian Boltanski gave a talk at the Art Institute of Chicago on December 8, 2015. "I am a dead artist" was written during this talk.

The poems in "documenta 13 daybook" include too many visitors and artworks to mention. I hope the titles act as clues.

Two encounters from February 21, 2015, inform "The absence of a body": Alejandro Figueredo Diaz-Perera's installation "In the absence of a body" at Chicago Artist Coalition, and a talk by Doris Salcedo at the Museum of Contemporary Art Chicago. For "In the absence…," Alejandro lived behind a wall in the gallery for a month, speaking to no one, taking food via a vent. Salcedo spoke of the disappeared.

The opening line of "Inhibition" paraphrases a passage of a letter from the chef David Murphy.

Susy and I found a photo of "The country's only open-air marble dance floor" while researching hotels, which have informed our collaborative art practice.

"Our fortunes our friends" was written for the wedding of Karl Wurst and Jennifer Golonka, which took place as the leaves turned in upstate New York.

"Cloudless" was written during two performances of choreographer Susan Marshall's evening-length work "Cloudless" six months apart. Marshall's works are lovely visual poems.

ACKNOWLEDGEMENTS

I am grateful to the editors of *Absent, Another Chicago Magazine, A Public Space, The Blue Letter, Chicago Artist Resource, Conduit, La familia Americana, Forklift, Ohio, Handsome, H_NGM_N, jubilat, LUNGFULL!, Pinwheel, Spinning Jenny,* and *Zoland Poetry,* where versions of some of the poems in this book appeared.

My deepest gratitude to the many people who have helped this book come into the world. Foremost to Susy Bielak, whose love, partnership, and faith keep me going. Most eternal thanks to Sarah Fox for her unerring eyes and ears, and unshakable friendship. To Daniel Borzutzky, G.E. Patterson, and Frances Richard for their deep reads and musical responses to the book. Thanks to the many friends and colleagues who read and commented on this work as it took shape. Paula Cisewski, Rachel Galvin, and Marwa Helal picked apart the manuscript and offered their expertise—it is a better book because of their care. To my parents, sisters, and brother for the upbringings. To Cara Megan Lewis, Alejandro Figueredo Díaz-Perera, Jenny Browne, Debby Bielak, and Elizabeth Zuba, for friendships and conversations. To Eric Kjensrud, Babette Tischleder, and Marleen Knipping, who remind me every day to be rigorous and different.

To Alex Yudzon for cover art and counter offers covered in feathers. Thanks to Anastasia Tinari for putting us in touch. To the incomparable Deb Sokolow for sharing without hesitation an artwork that brings wit and bite to the proceedings.

129

To Kazim Ali, Stephen Motika, and Lindsey Boldt for watching this work grow for years and saying yes when it was ready. Their attention and generosity as publishers has been inspiring to encounter. Thank you to Adam Bohannon for his sharp design.

Finally, to the artists whose work and conversations filtered into the poems both explicitly and implicitly, my utmost respect and thanks.

FRED SCHMALZ is an artist and writer whose current writing responds to encounters with art. Balas & Wax is his ongoing collaborative art practice with Susy Bielak. He lives in Chicago.